ALBERT VANHOYE

OUR PRIEST IS CHRIST

The Doctrine of the Epistle to the Hebrews

P. I. B.

Roma 1977

ALBERT VANHOYE S. J., *Le Christ est notre prêtre,* Supplément à « Vie chrétienne » n° 118 (Paris 1969), translated by Sister M. Innocentia Richards.

PREFACE

THE PRIESTHOOD

In our days the meaning of priesthood is questioned. The Council reminded Christians that they were all priests, because they participate in the priesthood of Christ (The Dogmatic Constitution of the Church, "Lumen Gentium", 10, 11, 34). It is clear that this doctrine calls for serious study.

Moreover, today the function of priests is questioned and society demands on their part an intense renewal. If they do not wish to wander in wrong directions, priests must, first of all, be sure of the doctrinal basis of their vocation.

The following pages do not pretend to point out a solution for all the contemporary problems. They are intended to help others draw near to the source of light, which, in this instance, is Christ the Priest. We cannot have a correct idea of the priesthood common to all Christians, or of the ministerial function of priests, if, first of all, we do not have a better understanding of the priesthood of Christ himself.

* * *

The New Testament assists us in our quest by presenting, over and above references scattered here and there, a magnificent text which in its entirety treats this aspect of the mystery of Christ. This text is not easy to handle. Its title reveals nothing of its content and does not seem attractive. The "Epistle to the Hebrews" is the text in question. Why should a Christian read the "Epistle to the Hebrews"? Indeed it would be better to use neither "epistle" nor "to the Hebrews", because the author speaks rather than writes and he speaks to Christians. Were we to choose a title that would more clearly indicate its content, we would have to say "the Priesthood of Christ" and then point out that its message is addressed "to bewildered Christians".

From what the author presents, it is clear that the Christians to whom he speaks were living in difficult times. From the period of their conversion they had "endured many painful trials" (10,32), imprisonment, the confiscation of their goods, diverse vexations, as had so many of their brothers in the newly founded churches (cf. 1 Th. 2,14). Years had gone by (Heb. 5,12), but the situation was again becoming threatening and they were becoming weary (12,3-4.12). Added to this, they had some doubts about matters of faith and religious practices (13,9; cf. 3,6; 4,14; 10,22-25).

It was necessary not only to restore confidence to these bewildered Christians, but it was also essential to provide opportunities for the acquisition of deeper doctrinal depth. When trial has dried up the springs from which one previously had drawn refreshment, it becomes necessary to dig more deeply in order to find again springs of living water. This explains why the author decides to go beyond the ordinary themes used in preaching (6,1) and to propose a more detailed explanation that would bring out a new point of view, namely, that of the priesthood of Christ.

His originality certainly does not consist in rejecting anything whatever of the traditional teaching on the passion and glorification of Our Lord. On the contrary, he retains carefully all these elements: sufferings and humiliations (2,10; 12,2-3), redeeming obedience (5,8; 10,5-9) on the one hand; and on the other hand, victory over death (2,14; 13,20), ascension into heaven (4,14; 9,24), the Lord's place at the right hand of God (1,3; 8,1; 12,2). However, he presents all the content of faith in a new synthesis, which, as we shall see, produces an increase of light.

1. AN ATYPICAL EPISTLE

Before considering the text of the epistle, the reader doubtless would like to have information about it; to know for example, the name of the author, the date of its composition and the place for which it was intended. Unfortunately, it is very difficult to give answers to all these questions.

On one point, at least, and it is an essential point, there is no doubt. The Church that presents this text assures us that it is a part of the Bible. The epistle to the Hebrews is an inspired writing, received as such by Christians; it is God's word spoken to man. More precisely it transmits to us along with other writings in the New Testament the authentic revelation of Jesus Christ. On this point, for many centuries there has been complete certitude in both the Eastern and Western Church.

The most solemn document on this subject is the decree of the Council of Trent, April 8, 1546, which defines the official list of the sacred books or what we call the "canon of the Scriptures". The epistle to the Hebrews is named there explicitly. Obviously, this decree was not innovative. It did nothing more than record a tradition that had been affirmed for a millenium and to which many anterior texts testify.

* * *

In this canonical list the Epistle to the Hebrews is placed with the epistles of Saint Paul. With the guarantee of Apostolic authority it is received by the Church, exactly as the other writings of the New Testament.

In this matter it must be noted that there are for the sacred books of the New Testament several possible ways of being "apostolic". The gospels according to the evangelists Mark and Luke are recognized by the Church as authentic testimony of the Apostles, without being considered books composed by an apostle. In the canon of Scripture the place assigned to the Epistle to the

Hebrews lets us see that this writing is not connected with Saint Paul in the same way as are the other Pauline epistles. It is named last, although its length and its importance might have led to its being placed near the beginning, close to the Epistle to the Romans.

It is easily seen that the Epistle to the Hebrews is in a class by itself. It is not introduced in the manner of a letter of Saint Paul. Paul's name is not mentioned, nor are the titles of the apostle. There is no mention of those for whom it is destined and the customary greeting is not found. In the other Pauline epistles we find the above elements.

The epistle does not begin like a letter, but like a carefully composed sermon. He who preaches does not have to give his name. He is seen and that suffices. He sees those to whom he speaks. This explains why he can launch into his subject immediately. This is the sort of beginning found in Hebrews 1,1-4. The author does not give his name. His only thought is to introduce the subject he is going to present.

The developments that follow completely confirm this first impression. Several times the author states that he is speaking; at no time does he say that he is writing. His way of expressing himself corresponds to that of a preacher who is speaking to his audience. In what he says we find nothing characteristic of the epistolary genre. His sermon is developed according to a well ordered plan. It shows skillful variations of tone, passing from doctrinal exposition to exhortation, yet retaining a certain gravity up to the concluding sentence (13,20-21), which ends with "amen".

However, a few lines are added (13,19.22-25). These are in epistolary style. The one writing them expresses himself more simply and uses the first person singular, "*I* ask you" (13,19.22), while the sermon regularly has the plural, "*we* have much to say" (5,11). The person writing these lines gives some news, expresses the hope of a future meeting, and sends the customary greetings. According to all appearances these lines constitute a short note added to the sermon when it was decided to send it to a distant Christian community.

The style of the sermon in no way resembles Saint Paul's style; its author is a person of very different temperament. In the measure that Saint Paul is spontaneous and impassioned, this author is reserved and moderate. Saint Paul, very conscious of his apostolic authority, forcefully states his own position in the Church; this author, on the contrary, maintains a marked reserve about himself. Saint Paul shows little care about writing well, and there is always a sort of improvisation when he develops his subject; this author composed his sermon skillfully.

Nevertheless, the most ancient testimony attributes the Epistle to the Hebrews to Saint Paul. The attribution rests on a tradition firmly rooted in the Eastern churches, and it cannot be set aside. How must it be understood? In the third century Origen proposed a solution that called for a distinction between Pauline origin, and redaction properly so called. According to his view, "the thoughts are those of the apostle", but "the expression and composition are by someone who reported the apostolic teachings". Origen acknowledged his ignorance in regard to the identity of the author. Others have adduced the names of Saint Luke, Clement of Rome and Barnabas.

Modern writers propose other names, in particular that of Apollo, the Alexandrian Jew mentioned in the Acts of the Apostles as well as in two epistles of Saint Paul. Having become a Christian, Apollo had placed his oratorical gifts and his knowledge of the Bible at the service of his faith (Act. 18,24-28; I Cor. 3,4-6; 16,12; Titus 3,13). What we know about him permits us to attribute with some likelihood the composition of the Epistle to the Hebrews to him, but on this point we are unable to be certain.

The distinction that there is reason to make between the two parts of the writing (a long sermon, followed by a short note), opens the door to an hypothesis that would take into consideration all the facts. We can believe that the two parts are not written by the same hand and that the sermon is the work of Apollo or another companion of Saint Paul, while the note, in a different style, could have been written by Saint Paul himself at the time of sending the written sermon elsewhere. The apostle would in this way have vouched for it. We know that Saint Paul, after having dictated his own epistles, would add a few words in his own hand (2 Thess. 3,17; 1 Cor. 16,21); it was easy to recognize his writing (Gal. 5,11).

Regardless of these hypotheses, the observable similarities between the doctrine of the Epistle to the Hebrews and the teaching of Saint Paul, particularly that found in the epistles of the captivity, support sufficiently the tradition of Pauline provenance.

* * *

We do not know with certainty for what audience the sermon was composed, nor to what community it was sent later. The traditional title, *"To the Hebrews"*, is not an integral part of the work. It was attached to it very early, its meaning remaining vague. The title may indicate that the sermon was addressed to groups strongly marked by a Judeo-Christian influence. In the first century this was the most frequent situation.

The only indication of place, found in the note (13,24), is for us as puzzling as possible. We read "those of Italy greet you". From these words we do not know whether the sender was in Italy or elsewhere, and they reveal nothing certain about the place to which the matter was sent.

As for the date, it seems necessary to place it in the years preceding the destruction of the temple at Jerusalem in the year 70, since the author refers to the temple liturgy as still being in existence (Heb. 10,1-3). These are the years during which the martyrdom of Saint Paul is placed.

Finally, we must be resigned to much uncertainty concerning the exact circumstances in which the epistle to the Hebrews was composed. For our purpose these questions are secondary. What is important is the content of the epistle, so rich in doctrinal teaching.

2. OVERVIEW

As we have already stated, the author composed his sermon with great care. Between the exordium (1,1-4) and the peroration (13,20-21), he divided it into five major parts. Each part is announced in sequence: the first in 1,4; the second in 2,17-18; the third in 5,9-10; the fourth in 10,36-39; the last in 12,13. Various indications bring out the successive limits of the developments to follow.

1. At the end of the exordium a commentary on the *"name"* of Christ, a name *"very different from that of the angels"*, is announced (1,4). In other words, the author is preparing to define Christ's position in relation to God and to men. This is the content of the first part: 1,5 - 2,18.

2. At the end of the above subject, the theme of the priesthood is introduced. Christ has become *"the merciful high-priest, worthy of faith"* (2,17). This is the content of the second part: 3,1 - 5,10.

3. In 5,9-10 new developments are announced and these go more deeply into the same theme. By his sacrifice, Christ became the cause of salvation. He was proclaimed a priest, not in the manner of the Jewish priests, but in a new way. These statements form the content of the third part (5,11 - 10,39), and bring out the differences between the high-priesthood of Christ and the ancient priesthood.

4. At the end of the third part (10,36-39), the author invites the Christians to remain united to Christ the Priest by remaining steadfast in trials and by keeping the faith, regardless of everything. This is the subject of the fourth part: 11,1 - 12,13.

5. In 12,13, he invites them to map out for themselves *"very straight paths"*. This is the subject of the fifth part (12,14 - 13,18), that will require each one to go forward toward peace and sanctity (12,14).

The following schema shows the sermon as a whole:

Introduction: 1,1-4.

  I. Christ's situation: 1,5 - 2,18.

  II. The first presentation of Christ's high-priesthood:
          3,1 - 5,10.

  III. Specific characteristics of Christ's high-priesthood:
          5,11 - 10,39.

  IV. Fidelity to Christ through persevering faith:
          11,1 - 12,13.

  V. Orientations for Christian life:
          12,14 - 13,18.

Conclusion: 13,20-21.

This schema simplifies things. It does not show well and in detail the place that counsels, warnings and words of encouragement given to the Christians have in the sermon. The author never forgets that the word of God is the seed of life. Accordingly, he is not satisfied with theoretical considerations, but tries continually to make faith enter into the whole of life. At the beginning of chapter two he calls on Christians to face up to their responsibilities (2,1-4). He returns to the charge in chapters three and four. Two urgent exhortations (5,11 - 6,20 and 10,19-39) set off his great central teaching. The mediation of Christ the Priest is not a shallow idea; it is a living reality that wants to become effective in our life.

The schema does not show how the author develops the mediation theme. In each part he brings out sequentially two aspects of the mystery, the idea of mediation in relation to God and then in relation to man. The glorified Christ is recognized as the Son of God (1,5-14); he is also the brother of men (2,5-18). This twofold relationship makes him a high priest. The complete union of these two aspects is brought about by one act, the personal sacrifice of Jesus Christ, a self-offering made to God for the salvation of men. In their turn, Christians in their lives are called upon to join faith (that places them close to God), with fellowship that unites them with their brothers.

Finally, it must be noted that to show better the revelation of Christ, the author continually makes comparisons with the Old Testament. His procedure is in no way an over-simplification. Quite the contrary; he is careful to point out several sorts of relationship. At one time he shows the continuity between the Old and the New Testaments; at other times he insists on the differences, and stresses more markedly that in the New Testament we pass to a higher plane. Resemblances, differences, superiority; such are the three relationships that must be noted in regard to Christ's high-priesthood when compared with the ancient worship. It is in this manner that Christian fulfillment is defined.

The pages that follow are intended to assist the reader in grasping the teaching found in the Epistle to the Hebrews. They will follow the general outline of the work. A significant exception will be the exhortation found in chapters three and four ("a warning against incredulity"); this matter will be handled along with chapter eleven ("examples of faith given by the ancients"). All the important themes will be studied in sequence. This procedure will give an idea of the doctrinal richness contained in this New Testament writing and will throw light on the problems of our times.

* * *

For a more fruitful reading of the Epistle to the Hebrews a detailed outline will be useful. One follows, and it will support the statements that have been made above. The titles used will permit us to follow the interchange of explanations and exhortations. *A* will indicate the developments in relation to God; *B* those that deal more with the affairs of men. The *comparisons* used by the author will be italicized.

OUTLINE OF THE EPISTLE

Exordium: Divine intervention in human history 1,1-4

Part I: Christ's situation 1,5 - 2,18
(*compared with the angels*)

    A. Son of God enthroned as King (1,5-14)

    — Exhortation to recognize his authority (2,1-4)

    B. His fellowship with men,
    acquired through the Passion (2,5-18)

Part II: Christ presented as our high priest 3,1 - 5,10

    A. Jesus, a high priest worthy of our faith
    because he is the Son of God (3,1-6)
    (*compared with Moses*)

    — Warning against incredulity and a call to
    carry out a heaven-sent vocation (3,7 - 4,14)
    (*Christ's companions compared with those of
    Moses and Joshuah*)

    B. Jesus, a high priest who has compassion on men
    and who fulfills his role through the Passion (4,15 -
    5,10)
    (*compared with Aaron*)

Part III: Specific characteristics of Christ's priesthood 5,11 - 10,39

    — An appeal for attention and generosity (5,11 - 6,20)
    (*compared with Abraham*)

    A. The glorious priesthood of the Son of God (7,1-28)
    (*relationship with Melchizedek, contrasted with
    Aaron*)

A-B. Main synthesis: the fulfillment of the priesthood due to the personal sacrifice through which Christ the mediator rises up to God (8,1 - 9,28) (*compared with the ancient sacrifices*)

B. Efficacy of Christ's sacrifice in face of men's sins (10,1-18) (*contrasted with the powerlessness of the ancient religion*)

— The call to draw near to God through Christ (10, 19-39) (*compared with the law of Moses*)

Part IV: Adherence to Christ through persevering faith 11,1 - 12,13

A. Examples of faith in God, shown by the ancients (11,1-40) (*compared with the mystery of Christ*)

B. Call to remain firm among men as did Jesus and to accept divine education through suffering (12,1-13) (*compared with human education*)

Part V: Orientation of Christian life 12,14 - 13,18.
(*compared with the religious situation as seen in the Old Testament*)

A. Relationship to be maintained in regard to heavenly realities (12,14-29)

— Definite directives (13,1-6)

B. Mutual dependence in the Church, centered in Christ's Passion (13,7-18).

Conclusion: Let God act in you through Jesus Christ! 13,20-21.

3. GOD HAS SPOKEN TO US

Hebrews 1,1-2

The opening words of the epistle to the Hebrews fix our attention on the word of God. The solemn style of the sentence, the author's care in balancing its varied elements, underscore the importance of the statement: *"In many and various ways God spoke of old to our fathers by the prophets; but in these last days he has spoken to us by a Son..."* A similar insistence will be found more than once in the epistle (2,1-4; 3,7 - 4,13; 12,25-29).

This is the essential fact. God has spoken. Note that the verb used has no direct object. Here, the author is not interested in the content of the message. It is not his intention to enumerate a list of truths we must believe in order to be saved. He is much more interested in the person who has spoken and he remains in his presence with profound respect. This is the fitting attitude. Indeed, Christian faith is not the adherence to a system of abstract ideas impersonnally proposed to human intelligence. The Bible is not a handbook devised for the dissemination of an "ideology". It is a word from someone addressed to someone, a word that cannot be separated from him who pronounces it. Therefore, it is a "living word" (4,12), summoning each of us.

God who speaks is worthy of our listening, our believing, and our docility (3,7; 3,12; 4,11)! Could one imagine a more *accredited* word? Since his word touches us more deeply than all human speech, touches the conscience and lays bare our narrowness, — "discerning the dispositions and thoughts of the heart" (4,12), — questions us making us feel helpless in view of its demands, we are tempted not to listen (12,25). Several times the author of the epistle warns against this deplorable manner of acting, capable of ruining a life. "Therefore, we must pay closer attention to what we have heard, lest we drift away" (2,1). The warning of Psalm 95 is repeated three times: "Today, when you hear his voice, do not harden your hearts ..." (3,7.15; 4,7).

Nothing is gained by being deaf to his word. It is possible to resist his authority for a time, but ultimately it is impossible to escape from him (2,2-3). Witness the fate of the stubborn Israelites, "whose bodies fell in the wilderness" (3,17; Numbers 14,29-33). God makes known the paths of true life (12,9); he who thinks to disregard this teaching surrenders to "the deceitfulness of sin" (3,13), goes astray and falls. The man of faith guides his course by the authority of the message received, as Abraham did. When God called, "he went out, not knowing where he was to go" (11,8).

He who starts out is not alone; he is *in touch* with God. God's word is not simply an order imposed on us. His message is not to be put on a par with that of a leader who from afar organizes a plan. God spoke to us because he willed to be in touch with us. Speaking is a way to have a person to person communication with another. The Samaritan woman knew this very well. She was astonished to hear Jesus make a request: "How is it that you, a Jew, ask a drink of me, a woman of Samaria?" "For Jews have no dealings with Samaritans", explains John (Jn 4,10). There are persons who no longer speak to one another because once they considered themselves offended. There are others who think it is beneath them to deal with certain categories of persons. They do not speak to them because they are on a lower social level. How different is the divine attitude! God has not scorned us because of our unimportance. Whatever our offenses may have been, God has not cut us off from his friendship and he still speaks to us.

He has not been satisfied with calling us once or twice like a lawyer who would send the customary summons. Resembling a father who trains his children, he has begun again "*many times*" (1,1), and "*persistently*" (Jeremias 7,15), endeavoring to find ways of reaching us, speaking "*in various ways*» (1,1). Sometimes he commanded, at other times he made promises, now punishing the rebellious or comforting the suffering, making use of every resource of human speech, and even shaping events — for God speaks also by deeds. In this way he has made known to us his plans and has made himself known, opening his heart to us.

Since it was a matter of establishing a relationship between God and man, all the varied aspects of the word of God join together so as to form a long *history*. God did not send to man a message outside the framework of time; he took the trouble to patiently fit his message into each one's day to day existence. Each message is marked by the circumstances that brought it about, often the Bible points them out and shows us the stages of the divine intervention. The author of the epistle sums up these stages in time by mentioning the times "*of old*" and "*the last days*" that bring about the great accomplishment.

The word of God is also historical because it is addressed to men as free beings whose choices influence history. By speaking to us God intends to associate us freely with his work. His work brings about decisions that change the course of events, and it leads us to a true, living participation in God's life. This is, moreover, the profound reason for its exigency.

To make all this possible, God must find out how his message can be delivered. Men speak the language of men. It is through living men that the living word is to be transmitted, establishing in this way a relationship among them. So that his word might enter into human life, God asked men for their voices. In truth he asked for more than their voices! The message dwelling "*in the prophets*" (1,1) demanded their hearts and their lives so that it might be proclaimed. This indwelling message was not an undemanding guest. If it brought them joy, it also brought them torment, causing struggle within and round about them (cf. Jer. 15,16; 20,9).

It was clear that God's word in them was constricted and could only be expressed partially (the literal meaning of the first word in 1,1 is "in numerous divisions"). Speaking through the prophets God made himself known, but indirectly. He was entering into our lives, but through intermediaries. The relationship achieved through the prophets' words remained remote and imperfect. It only aroused a greater longing for a more realistic meeting: "O that thou wouldst rend the heavens and come down ..." (Isaiah 64,1).

Actually, a more realistic meeting was being prepared (cf. Is. 52,6), the meeting accomplished "*in the Son*". No longer was it to be a man exterior to God who would speak to us, but a divine person whose unity with the Father is expressed in the strongest terms the author can find: "*He reflects the glory of*

God and bears the very stamp of his nature" (1,3), and who will be named God and Lord: *"But of the Son he says, Thy throne, O God"* ... (1,8-9); *"And, Thou, Lord"* ... (1,10). It was not enough for God to speak to us by borrowing our language. Wishing to transfigure our lives by granting us the power to communicate among ourselves and with him (1 Jn. 1,3), he came in the person of Jesus Christ to share our life and to speak not simply the language of words, but also the language of a life offered and of blood outpoured.

Such is the result of God's word. In Jesus Christ it reaches its apogee under all aspects: authority, revelation, historical development, and above all, the aspect of the relationship between God and us: Jesus is *"the mediator of a new covenant"*, (9,15); his blood *"speaks more strongly than the blood of Abel"* (Heb. 12,24).

4. A NAME MORE EXCELLENT THAN THAT OF THE ANGELS

Hebrews 1,4 - 2,16

At the far end of an underground passage, blocked by fallen earth, the workmen at Champagnole, filled with anguish, were wondering if they would ever again see light. The first sounds that reached them from the outside raised their hopes, for they put them into communication with the living. Although the anguish is not ordinarily experienced in such a dramatic way, nevertheless, it is in a somewhat analogous situation that the word of God reaches men. Without God's word, would we not be like living persons entombed, surrounded by the darkness of death (Lk. 1,79), unable to trace a path of life? When God's word reaches us our distress is mitigated, we have hope. Nevertheless, the first divine initiative is but a beginning. Communication once established, the problem of rescue remains. Words are not sufficient to effect this; the rescuer must pay in person. Accordingly, God himself undertook to rescue us in the person of his Son, Jesus Christ.

The prologue of the Epistle to the Hebrews, begun by evoking the divine word, ends by insisting on the personal intervention of the Son of God and on the result of this intervention: *"... When he had made the purification for sins, he sat down at the right hand of the Majesty on high, having become as much superior to angels as the name he has obtained is more excellent than theirs"* (Heb. 1,3-4). In these few words the author resumes the whole mystery of Christ. In the course of the epistle he will return to this idea several times to show its richness from different points of view, but his glance will be fixed on the person of Jesus (2,9; 3,1; 12,2). To strengthen the persecuted Christians, to encourage those dogged by weariness, he knows there is nothing so potent as the contemplation of Jesus.

At this point the author's manner of expressing his mind may seem disconcerting. Why, suddenly speak about angels? Why such insistance on the "name"? These unanticipated expressions prepare the whole development that is to follow (1,5 - 2,18). In these two chapters the writer continually compares Christ to the angels. By degrees he will adduce all the elements necessary to define the name he has invoked. By defining it, he will, at the same time, ascertain the religious condition of the Christians.

If he writes so much about the angels, it is because many persons in those times of uncertainty and religious emotion, imagined that the surest way to get in touch with God was to approach him through the angels. Are they not the closest beings to God, those to whom he confided the duty of praising him in heaven itself? Furthermore, to them was attributed the cosmological role of regulating the stars, the equilibrium of the elements, in such a manner that life on earth depended on them. All the greater reason to think the intervention of angels would be significant in obtaining man's salvation. This conviction is often expressed in the *Dead Sea* scrolls.

The resultant "cult of the angels" was reprehended by Saint Paul in Col. 2,18. This cult was an attractive mixture of false mysticism and religious formalism. It excited the imagination by evoking brilliant, heavenly liturgies or prestigious earthly victories. By attributing absolute value to concrete observances a feeling of moral security was obtained.

Since the angels regulated the course of the stars, it was necessary to submit strictly to the prescriptions of a certain calendar, to note the *days, months, seasons* and *years* (Gal. 4,10). In order to respect the *elements* it was necessary to follow the minute rules of ritual purity (Col. 2,16.20-21). Truly, such religious behavior, in its dualistic aspect, was a dual rejection of existence. It gave man only an illusion of salvation and brought no authentic progress towards God. Far from encouraging it, Christ's apostles straightway fought it and unmasked it. Indeed the revelation of Christ is the direct opposite of this sort of religiosity. The name of Christ is something very different from the name of angels.

The author's insistence on the "*name*" shows clearly that he does not understand the term in a merely superficial sense. For us, a person's name is simply a word chosen arbitrarily to point him out, a convenient social convention. The ancient author is more attentive to the meaning of the name, to the image of the person whom the name would evoke. The name is considered as expressing the ensemble of qualities, aptitudes and powers of the one named. The name points up the person's position, his personal value and dignity. This is why a hierarchy of names exists (Eph. 1,21).

This first aspect necessarily calls to our attention another very important one in this context. The name is a means of connection between persons and determines the nature and extent of their relationships. To be able to call someone, his name or a suitable title must be known. To a given level of relationship there is a corresponding appellation; it may be distant or familiar, polite or free and easy, a title, a given name or a surname. Obviously, the two aspects mentioned are closely related.

When the writer recalls the name Christ received, it is the position of Christ that he wishes us to consider and the nature of his relationship with God and with us. This position, he says, is very different from that of the angels, and signifies that Christ "*is worth much more than they.*" Why? Two reasons are shown: Christ is closer to God than the angels are (1,5-14). Christ is also closer to us (2,5-11). As a matter of fact, his name is both that of the Son of God (1,5) and also that of the brother of men (2,11-12).

For these two reasons, Christ is worth much more than the angels; the communication that we can have with God through him is more intimate and lasting. This communication does not pass through a remote intermediary half-way between God and us, but is fixed in the unity of the same person.

The very concise statement in verse 3 recalls how Christ obtained this name: "*Having accomplished the purification from sins, he took his place at the right hand of Majesty.*" The author thus established his developmental perspective. He is not fixing his gaze on the Word of God before the Incarnation, nor is it fixed on the child at Bethlehem; it is fixed on Christ sacrificed, who through his sacrifice entered into the glory of the Father.

It is in Christ sacrificed and glorified that the inspired words of Psalm 2, quoted in Heb. 1,5, are fully verified: "*You are my son, today I have begotten you*" (Ps. 2,7). This prophecy pointed to the king of Israel, anointed in Sion (Ps. 2,6), the Messiah of God (Ps. 2,2). It is fulfilled with unimaginable completeness in the mystery of the resurrection, when the human nature of Christ, son of David, is wholly transformed and penetrated with the glory of the Son of God (Jn. 17,5). Until that time, Jesus came in the form of a servant (Phil. 2,7). His sacrifice accomplished, he receives in his humanity *the name* which is above every name (Phil. 2,9).

Nothing similar can be, or will ever be affirmed of the angels. The Bible shows that angels, however close to God they may be, have a subordinate position, and the great renewal announced in the prophetic texts in no way changes their condition.

The objection may be raised that if Christ is closer to God, he is by that very fact farther from us. Not at all, because the mystery of the glorified Christ has a twofold aspect. His sacrifice, which, as we have just stated, is the way that led him to the glory of the Father, has also the effect of manifesting and strengthening his solidarity with us.

It must be noted that Jesus begins his life in a situation *"lower than the angels"* (2,9), in other words right on our level. His upward way begins in the very midst of our natural obscurity and for that very reason he is truly *"the pioneer of our salvation"* (2,9). He was not satisfied with giving us directives from heaven to be followed; having come among us, he began to show us the way; his present position at the right hand of the Father assures us that *"a new and living way"* has been pointed out to us, a way that will lead us to God.

There is yet more. The glorification of Jesus might have been presented to us as a sort of evasion outside the frame of the human condition. Rather his glorification is based on the complete acceptance of the realities of our life, including the most painful ones, suffering and death (2,10). Not only is it because of *"having suffered death"* that Jesus is now *"crowned with glory and honor"* (2,9), it is *"through"* these very *"sufferings"* that he has *"been made perfect"* (2,10; 5,8-9). In the face of suffering and death, human beliefs and ideologies are all, more or less explicitly, doctrines of escape, marxism not excluded. No doctrine of escape is worthy of God. God does not shirk reality. Therefore, Christ took our painful condition and made of it the way of true life. He did not remove its burdens, but imbuing it with new values, he transformed it. Because he freely accepted suffering and death, prompted by loving docility to his Father (10,5-10) and brotherly solidarity with us (2,10-15), he gave them a positive meaning and made them instruments of redemption. Therefore, *"through suffering"* his humanity was transformed and raised to the full glory of Sonship.

At the same time, it is clear that his glorification, far from separating him from us, seals his union with us. Glorified, he calls us his *"brothers"* (2,11); indeed, it is because he showed himself our brother to the very end that he has been crowned; he has been glorified because his love for us knew no bounds (Jn 13,1), giving as he did his life for us. When he is glorified, it is his humanity that is *"crowned with glory and honor."* In Christ enthroned, man's vocation finds its first accomplishment in a manner surpassing anything that could have been conceived (2,5-9).

Therefore the glorious Christ, one with the Father, is nevertheless, closer to us than the angels. His name is not only *Son of God, God* and *Lord*; it is also *man* and *son of man* (2,6), *Jesus,* (2,9), *pioneer of our salvation* (2,10), who *does not blush to call us his brothers* (2,11), we, the *little children* confided to him by God (2,13). The path he marks out for us is not then to be found either in the realms of mythical imagination nor in the areas of irrational cults; it cuts through the realities of human life, filling it with authentic value. It is not an illusory salvation.

5. A MERCIFUL AND TRUSTWORTHY HIGHPRIEST

Hebrews 2,17-18; 3,1 - 5,10

The great originality of the Epistle to the Hebrews is that it, alone among all the writings of the New Testament, applies to Christ the title of priest and high priest. In the gospels, the other epistles, the Apocalypse, we do not find Jesus so designated. In the Epistle to the Hebrews, it is his most frequent title. The importance attributed to this title is shown by the place where it is used for the first time, at the conclusion of the explanation of the "name" of Christ. After having shown Christ's position in relation to the Father (1,5-14) and his solidarity with us (2,5-16), the writer concludes: *"Therefore he had to be made like his brethren in every respect, so that he might become a merciful and trustworthy high priest in the service of God, to make expiation for the sins of the people"* (Heb. 2,17). In this way the author prepares the second part of his explanation, which will introduce Christ as a trustworthy (3,1-6) and merciful high priest (4,15 - 5,10). In the third part (5,11 - 10,39), a long chapter (7,1-28) will again be given to defining the priesthood of Christ.

This insistence is easily understood if we recall that the central theme of the epistle is the question of our approach to God. How can we enter into contact with God? How can we live in union with him? In short, how can we have a religious life marked by the sign of authenticity? The answer is that in order to draw near to God, we must offer him true worship and there can be no genuine worship without a priest worthy of this name. Is this condition fulfilled in Christian life? At first sight, it might be doubted. Indeed, according to current ideas, Jesus was not a priest. He did not belong to the priestly class. Our author himself does not fail to note this: *" It is known that Our Lord is of the tribe of Juda, a tribe of which Moses said nothing when he speaks of the priests"* (7,14). John the Baptist belonged to a priestly family (Lc. 1,5), but Jesus did not. In the Gospel there is nothing on the part of Jesus to show he had any pretention of assuming any special role in the Jewish worship. Therefore, it is not surprising that the title of high priest was not accorded him in early Christian preaching.

To stop here would give proof of a superficial mind and a lack of understanding in relation to the "fulfillment" of the Scriptures. The revelation of Christ necessarily calls for a revision of current ideas. It goes beyond what was before. Enlightened by the light of Christ, our author studied all aspects of the idea of priesthood, and little by little realized that the position of Christ glorified, such as he had described it in replying to the Jewish high priest (Mt. 26,64) and such as it was recognized and proclaimed by the apostles after Pentecost (Act. 2,33-34), is indeed the position of the perfect high priest. It is to this same discovery that the author leads his reader in the first part of the epistle.

What is necessary in order to be a high priest? First and above all, it is necessary to be accepted by God, to be admitted into his presence. The function of the priest is specifically that of a mediator before God and it is he who is to assure communication with God. By whom is this first condition better fulfilled than by Christ enthroned at the right hand of God and proclaimed Son of God?

There is an additional condition: genuine solidarity must unite the priest to those whom he represents before God. Were it otherwise, it is clear that the desired communication could not be firmly established. Christ having made himself our brother even unto dying on the cross, the second condition is fulfilled in him with consummate perfection.

Therefore the two aspects of the "name" of Christ correspond to the two exigencies of priesthood: union with God and union with men. Contemplating Christ, who through his passion seals his solidarity with us and through his passion enters into glory, the Christian recognizes an authentic priestly accomplishment. Christ has become "*high priest*."

Moreover, the attribution of this title is supported by the Scriptures. Psalm 110, which Jesus applied to himself when answering his judges, does not simply speak of his sitting at the Father's right hand; it also proclaims the priesthood of the enthroned Lord: *"You are a priest for ever after the order of Melchizedek"* (Ps. 110,4).

Let us notice the two expressions qualifying the title of high priest. They point up the twofold relationship already mentioned. *"Merciful"* recalls a brother's feeling for his brother and Jesus' solidarity with those who are afflicted. *"Trustworthy for the relationship with God"* reminds us of the status of the enthroned Christ. He is worthy of our faith, we can rely on him because the Father has placed all things in his hands. It is possible to see other shades of meaning, but these are the principal ones and the author bases his double-headed exhortation on them. 1) Since Jesus is worthy of our faith, let us place our faith in him (3,7 - 4,14): *"Since then we have a great high priest who has passed through the heavens, Jesus, the Son of God, let us hold fast our confession"* (Heb. 4,14; cf. 3,1-2). 2) Since Jesus is merciful, let us not fear to draw near to him: *"For we have not a high priest who is unable to sympathize with our weakness, but one who in every respect has been tempted as we are, yet without sinning. Let us then with confidence draw near to the throne of grace, that we may receive mercy and find grace to help in time of need"* (Heb. 4,15-16).

Therefore, a continuity between the Old Testament and the New Testament may be affirmed. The institution of priesthood did not end; it leads to, and is fulfilled in Christ's high priesthood. In a magnificent section, the author brilliantly brings out the parallelism between the former high priesthood and that of Christ (5,1-10). First, he defines the meaning of priesthood (5,1-4), and then makes the application to Christ (5,5-10).

Solidarity with men is the first characteristic mentioned: *"For every high priest chosen from among men is appointed to act on behalf of men in relation to God, to offer gifts and sacrifices for sins. He can deal gently with the ignorant and wayward, since he himself is beset with weakness"* (5,1-2). Indeed, such was Christ's situation. The author repeats it here, realistically, describing Jesus *"in the days of his flesh,"* with all that his struggle with death showed of his human weakness when he offered *"prayers and supplication with loud cries and tears, to him who was able to save him from death, and he was heard for his godly fear"* (5,7). The writer has no fear of affirming that Jesus, *"Al-*

though he was a Son, learned obedience through what he suffered" (5,8). Could a more genuine example of solidarity with men be thought of? We grasp the fact that in this manner "*Christ has become the source of salvation to all who obey him*" (5,9).

A second important characteristic to be noted is that admission to priesthood does not stem from man's initiative but from God's: "*And one does not take the honor upon himself, but he is called by God, just as Aaron was*" (5,4). It is the same in relation to Christ (5,5-6). "*So also Christ did not exalt himself to be made a high priest, but was appointed by him who said to him, 'Thou art my son, today I have begotten thee'; as he says in another place, 'Thou art a priest for ever, after the order of Melchizedek'*" (5,5-6).

There is also a third characteristic. The passing from human misery to the holiness of God is effected by a sacrificial act; the function the high priest is established for is "*to offer gifts and sacrifices for sins*" (5,1); he carries out this function for himself and for the people (5,3). This characteristic is verified in Christ's passion; he fulfilled this priestly role: "*Jesus offered up ., and was heard ... *". (5,8). In his human nature he truly carried the burden of our sins (2,14; Rom. 8,3). His offering was not for "his" sins, since he was sinless (4,15). Yet, it was for himself as well as for us. His sacrifice was consummated not solely to repair for our sins, but also, in accordance with God's plan (2,10), to transform the human nature he had assumed.

Therefore, all the attributes of priesthood are found in the mystery of Christ. We have in Jesus Christ a *high priest, merciful and trustworthy,* and thus we can, with unbounded hope, draw near to God.

6. A MODIFIED PRIESTHOOD

Hebrews 7,11-28

Meditating on the Scriptures in the light of the Passion and the Resurrection, the author of the Epistle to the Hebrews recognizes that the ancient priesthood attained its term in Jesus Christ and he shows us a correlation between Aaron and Christ through resemblance and continuity. This was pointed out in the preceding chapter. Nevertheless, this correlation does not fully define Christ's priesthood. Its Christian realization includes basic differences. Our author is fully aware of these differences and does not hesitate to speak of a *change in the priesthood* (7,12).

Let us note that this state of affairs is not peculiar to the priestly ministry. The same may be said of all the other components of the Christian realization. For example, let us consider the manner in which Jesus is the son and successor of David. Certainly, there is a real continuity (Lk. 1,32). However, the royal kingship of Jesus Christ was not accomplished in the manner expected. All ideas formed on this subject were subverted, refuted and exceeded. Christ's struggle did not conform to the pattern that had been foreseen (Ps. 45,4-6; cf. Mt. 26,51-54; Jn. 18,36) and his victory seemed to be a defeat (Lk. 24,21), but it was complete (Jn. 16,33; Heb. 2,14-15) and his triumph most glorious (12,2).

It is always thus when God completes what he has prepared for a long time. At first we have difficulty in recognizing this. A certain period of time is necessary so that our limited minds and narrow hearts may become adapted to a divine realization and to the brilliant light emanating from it. Or, it is necessary that the divine realization influence us, train and transform us. Only then, do we realize the varied relationships between the old and the new order of things, and we recognize (the Epistle to the Hebrews often brings this out) that these relationships are of three types. There is a genuine *continuity* (God does not lack coherence in his ideas); nevertheless, *differences* are noted and at certain points there are complete breaks, for it has been necessary to progress to a *higher level.* And what is true of the history of salvation, with due proportion safeguarded, is true also of the stages of our spiritual life.

In relation to the priesthood of Christ, the differences are not minimal. They are seen even in the passage that insists on the resemblances. The definition of high priest (5,1-4) and its application to Christ (5,5-10) do not correspond exactly when it is a matter of sacrificial activity. We shall treat this point later. Here, let us direct our attention to the position of the high priest in relation to men and to God.

* * *

The Old Testament hardly touches on the necessity of the priest being chosen from among men. That was self-evident. It insists, rather, on the necessity of separating the priest from other men. The priests are consecrated to God; therefore, they are not to remain on the same level as laymen. The ceremonies of ordination expressed this separation. After the ceremonial bath, intended to efface worldly contacts, the high priest was clothed with special garments and sacred vestments and he was anointed on the head with holy chrism and with several applications of the blood of the sacrifice (Ex. 29; Lv. 8-9).

The separation obtained in this manner was further guaranteed by numerous regulations. The rules concerning ritual purity were imposed strictly on the priests and above all, on the high priest. For example, he was forbidden to go near the body of any dead person, even were it the corpse of his own father (Lev. 21,11). Therefore, becoming a high priest implied that one elected to be different from others and that one was on a superior level. Looked upon as a promotion, the role of high priest gave rise to intrigues, above all when it tied in with political power. Towards the beginning of the Christian era, ambitious men used all possible means to obtain the position of high priest (2 Mac. 4,7.24).

In this context, the first statement of the epistle on the subject of the priesthood stands out like a paradoxical novelty. In order "*to become a high priest,*" it is not written that Christ had to separate himself from other men; on the contrary, we read that "*he had to become in all things like his brothers.*" In other words, he had to be tried and tempted (2,18; 4,15), to be insulted (11,26), to suffer (5,8) and to die (2,9).

The contrast stands out more markedly when the qualification of *the merciful one,* predicated of the high priest, is considered (2,17). In fact, several texts in the Bible seem to require severity more than mercy as being essential for the position of high priest. To be on God's side it is necessary to have the courage to stand up to sinners. In the desert when the people fall into idolatry, Moses ordered the Levites loyal to him to punish pitilessly, *to kill,* even though the victim might be a *brother, a friend, a neighbor.* This order carried out, Moses told them: "*Today, you have taken upon yourselves the investiture as priest of Jehovah, one at the cost of his son, another at the cost of his brother*" (Ex. 32,25-29). A similar episode is told of Phinehas, who, in an equally forceful intervention, won the dignity of high priest (Nb. 25). The blessing bestowed on the tribe of Levi supports this viewpoint; the priesthood requires detachment from all family ties (Dt. 33,8-11). The necessity of absolute fidelity to God is strikingly brought out. It would seem that this fidelity must exclude the slightest pity towards men.

Christ's priesthood shows us a very different picture. It is clear that Christ's fidelity to his Father did not require the breaking of his bonds with us. On the contrary, it led him to tighten the bonds of brotherhood with us and to push to the ultimate his love for and his solidarity with us. It was not by rising up against us that he became our high priest; he accomplished this by throwing in his lot with us. This was God's admirable plan. "*For it was fitting that he, for whom and by whom all things exist, in bringing many sons to glory, should make the pioneer of their salvation perfect through suffering*" (2,10).

We should not conclude that the struggle against sinful humanity required in the Old Testament was suddenly abandoned in the New Testament. It has not been abandoned. Rather, it has been continued in another radically new and efficacious manner. Christ is not to be compared with Phinehas who would kill his brothers in punishment for their having offended God. With love and with generous obedience, Christ underwent the death we merited. By doing this he changed the meaning of death.

Death was a result of and a punishment for sin; in Christ it became an act of supreme love. For the same reason, it was changed from being the gateway to loss to the gateway of glory. In the humanity of Christ, the battle ended in victory, God's and man's victory, a victory over sin and death: *"But we see Jesus, who for a little while was made lower than the angels, crowned with glory and honor because of the suffering of death, so that by the grace of God he might taste death for every one"* (2,9). Fidelity to God and solidarity with us could not be more closely united. Christ, the high priest, reveals to us the merciful love of the Father.

It is to be noted that mercy is not wholly missing in the biblical portrait of the high priest. A dramatic story describes the intervention of Aaron who, to save the people, stems the progress of a devastating calamity (Nb. 17,9-15; Sg. 18,20-25). However, this incident is a far cry from the intimate association of Christ's destiny with ours, effected by his death.

* * *

If we consider the position of the high priest in relation to God, the differences are clear. To express them, the author is guided by the divine proclamation of Psalm 110,4: *"The Lord has sworn and will not change his mind, 'You are a priest for ever after the order of Melchizedek'."* Christ, like Aaron, was named a priest by God (Heb. 5,4), but Christ's priesthood is not according to that of Aaron; *"it is according to Melchizedek"* (Heb. 5,4).

Following this indication, the author rereads the sentences in Genesis which treat of Melchizedek (Gn. 14,18-20; Heb. 7,1-3). Due to the manner in which Melchizedek is presented, the author has no difficulty in recognizing a prefiguration of the glorious Christ, king as well as priest, greater than Abraham (7,6-7; cf. Jn. 8,58) and, therefore, greater than all Jewish priests. Christ's sacerdotal power does not rest on his belonging to a priestly family. It is founded on his possession of eternal life (7,16), the life of the Son of God, the life, thanks to his Passion, that flowered in his glorified humanity (7,3.28). Consequently, the relationship of the glorified Christ with his Father incomparably surpasses that of the ancient high priests with God. The force of the expression found in the psalm when it speaks of a divine oath expresses this closer relationship, this definitive and "*better covenant*" (7,20-22).

Christ's priesthood is free from all the shortcomings that characterized the ancient priesthood. The Jewish priests were not appreciably changed after their consecration; after, as before it, their weaknesses remained (7,28). They were mortal and death brought an end to their functions (7,23). Ritually separated from sinners, they were actually sinners themselves who were not able to be intimate with God (9,8-10). Christ's humanity, through his glorifying Passion, was completely renewed. It can no longer be affected by weakness. The risen Christ dies no more, therefore his priesthood will never end and no stain will ever touch him (7,26).

The ritual requirement that the high priest be separated from men, as already observed, in Christ's case gave way to an admirable solidarity with man. However in a different sense this requirement was perfectly fulfilled in Christ, his humanity being, as Saint Paul says, dead to sin forever, and living unto God (Rom. 6,10). He is by this fact "*separated from sinners*" (7,26). Accordingly, he is "*for ever the perfectly consecrated*" high priest (7,28). Because his consecration was obtained by dying for us, he, nonetheless, belongs to us. Close to God, he remains close to us. He is *our* high priest.

What wonderment we experience in delving into this reality! "*For it was fitting that we should have such a high priest, holy, blameless, unstained, separated from sinners, exalted above the heavens.... Now the point in what we are saying is this: we have such a high priest, one who is seated at the right hand of the throne of the Majesty in heaven ...*" (7,26; 8,1). May God be praised for this ineffable gift!

7. THE ANCIENT OFFERINGS AND CHRIST'S SACRIFICE

Hebrews 8 - 10

According to the Epistle to the Hebrews, priesthood connotes an offering made to God. It states (5,1) and repeats (8,3) that *"every high priest is appointed to offer gifts and sacrifices."* This obligation is equally binding on Christ (8,3). Christ's priesthood was effected in a sacrificial offering. On this point, as on others, a concrete continuity is observed; in each instance it is a question of a bloody sacrifice. On this point more than on some others, there are very far reaching differences that completely change the perspective. It is important to point them out.

This subject is treated particularly in the central chapters of the epistle (8 - 10). A detailed comparison between the ancient practice and Christ's priestly activity is made there. There, and throughout the epistle, access to God is the major question. To this fundamental yearning, "O God, thou art my God, I seek thee, my soul thirsts for thee" (Ps. 63,2), there are obstacles. A weak and sinful people is aware of the distance separating it from a most holy God. The high priest's role is to bridge this gap and set up communication. The means by which he draws near to God must be an offering, through which is expressed his desire to be received.

Man is not simply far away from God. By sin he has offended God and stained himself; he is no longer in a state to appear before God. Along with the distance to be bridged, there is forgiveness to be obtained and purification to be effected.

How did the ancient religion face up to this situation? What was the significance of the high priest's action? Our author notes that it was on an earthly plane and limited to this plane. The sanctuary erected according to the prescriptions of the law could not really be the house of God because God does not dwell in man-made buildings. In fact, this sanctuary was only a symbol (8,5). And this symbol, by its arrangement and the liturgical laws governing the ceremonies, evidenced a negative meaning.

The Tent, as we find it in Exodus, like the temple at Jerusalem which came later, was divided into two parts. One part served as the sanctuary properly so called, the other part serving as a vestibule (9,2-4). Only the vestibule was generally accessible. Entry into the other part was governed by strict laws. Only the high priest, once a year, could enter it when he carried in sacrificial blood in order to make Expiation (9,7). After this solemn service the entrance to the sanctuary was closed. Our author remarks that this regulation, inspired by God, showed the inefficacy of the high priest's role. The purpose of his action was to establish communication between the people and God. Since at the end of the liturgy the same restrictions were imposed and the same inability recognized, it is clear that neither had communication been established nor had nearness to God been attained. The service was simply a sort of ineffective mime. The high priest did not open up a path to God (9,8).

This failure was due to the empty ritual. According to the author these actions were nothing but "the ritual of the flesh" (9,10), completely exterior. An essential distinction between the high priest and the sacrifices he offers must be noted: man cannot offer himself because he is unclean and therefore unworthy of being offered to God. Accordingly, the high priest must find a being that is not unclean, and he is instructed to find and offer an animal "without blemish."

Such "*gifts and sacrifices*" are incapable of obtaining the desired result, that of having the high priest himself rendered pleasing to God. Whatever may be the exterior perfection of the ceremonies, they cannot transform the interior of the person who offers them (9,9). "*It is impossible that the blood of bulls and goats should take away sin*" (10,4). The ancient cult, wholly exterior, did not renew man deeply and interiorly and therefore could not place him in real relationship with God.

Christ comes to remedy this ineffectual situation. How different will be his offering! Its marked newness is apparent even in the passage, 5,1-10, that aims to show the resemblances. Whereas the personal existence of the high priest and the rites he carries out are differentiated clearly (5,1-3), this distinction is not found in the text about Christ. Christ's offering cannot be separated from the drama of his life (5,7-8). The prayer that bursts forth in his combat with death is his offering. His very agony is his offering. These are not exterior ritual, they are the reality of life and death.

The contrast expressed here is underscored more forcefully later on. The author contrasts the high priests who *"offer gifts and sacrifices"* with Christ who *"offered himself"* (7,27; 9,9.14). The high priest enters the sanctuary with the blood of an animal (9,12.25); Christ enters into the sanctuary *"with his own blood"* (9,12).

His personal sacrifice was possible because, unlike the high priests, he was a victim *"without blemish"* (9,14). He was untouched by sin (4,15), although he had taken on himself the weakness of our nature and was in this way able to suffer for our sins. Therefore, Christ could *"offer himself to God"* and be accepted.

The absence of sin is not sufficient to bring out the value of sacrifice; an interior principle assuring the movement towards God must be added; in the fullness of the Spirit Christ offers himself (9,14). Seeing that the exteriority of the ancient sacrifices could not please God, he offers himself spontaneously to lovingly carry out the will of his Father: *"In burnt offerings and sin offerings thou hast taken no pleasure. Then I said, So, I have come to do thy will, O God"* (10,6.7).

This perfectly interior sacrifice was none the less real. It was not simply on the plane of intention, nor was it solely a symbolic expression. It took up human nature in its entirety and was fulfilled through human suffering and death. Here again there is something new. The ancient rite assigned no special value to the death of the victim and did not even mention suffering. Death was a foregone condition in relation to the offering and it was followed by the ritual properly so called (the action of offering, the rite of blood, and the burning of the victim). Christ's sacrifice consisted in his sufferings and his death.

It would be more exact to say that it consisted in the transformation of suffering and death. Death, as it was imposed on the sons of Adam, brought nothing good; it did but accentuate man's separation from God (Ps. 6,6; Is. 38,18).

The marvel of the mystery of Christ is that he assumed our death as sinners (which death would not lead to God); but freely assuming it through a movement of pure love for us and in perfect union with the love coming from the Father, he transformed death and made it a sacrifice that leads to God.

Death, transformed into a perfect sacrifice, is a death that opens up a new life, a life in communion with God, the life of the risen Christ. Let us note that resurrection is an integral part of perfect sacrifice, which could not consist simply in the destruction of the victim. Here, too, is something very new. Describing the former priesthood (5,1-4), the author does not comment on any effect of the sacrifice on the high priest himself; in later developments he explicitly denies any effect on him (7,19; 9,9; 10,1-3). In relation to Christ, the sacrifice led to the transformation of him who offered it. Christ was made perfect by his sufferings (2,10; 5,9), his humanity was completely consecrated (Jn. 17,19), completely penetrated with divine sanctity (Rom. 1,4), and truly risen. Resurrection is not to be understood as a simple biological miracle; it connotes spiritual transformation. Our author states that Christ *"learned obedience"* (5,8). His humanity is no longer that mortal flesh that bore the results of disobedience; it is a humanity rebuilt through the filial obedience of the cross and in which nothing any longer resists the God-life.

Because of this transformed humanity, the distance between God and man has been truly bridged. His risen body, *"a greater and more perfect tent, not made with hands"* (9,11), allows Christ to enter into the true sanctuary, *"not made with hands"* (9,24). His sacrifice is not restricted to an earthly level; it reaches *"to heaven itself"*, where Christ has entered in, now *"to appear in the presence of God on our behalf"* (9,24).

Thus, in Christ's sacrifice all is profoundly real. Our high priest truly took on our human condition, he truly sanctified it and raised it up to God in an unparalleled thrust of love.

3. THE MEDIATOR OF A NEW COVENANT

Hebrews 8,6-13; 9,15-23; 10,1-18

The sacrifice Christ offered was for him the path to glory. It was a supreme act of obedience and love that involved his human nature, causing it to pass through death in order to be remade according to the will of God. This sacrifice terminated in the Resurrection and the Ascension. *"We see Jesus ... crowned with glory and honor because of the suffering and death"* (2,9). *"Because he endured the cross, despising the shame, he is seated at the right hand of the throne of God"* (12,2). His humanity possesses all the glory which he had as Son of the Father before the world was made (Jn. 17,5.24). Therefore, the value of his sacrifice is evident.

The worth of his sacrifice is not limited to this aspect; it includes all humanity because Jesus died *for us*. To express this element of the mystery, the author of the epistle starts, as he always does, with the witness of the Old Testament: he shows how the covenant of God with his people was fulfilled in Christ. This fulfillment was underscored by Jesus' word at the Last Supper when he had offered his blood, shed for the multitude, as *"the blood of the covenant"* (Mt. 26,28). In virtue of this word, our author gives Christ the title of *"the mediator of a new covenant"* (9,15). The sanctifying death of Christ was a covenant sacrifice, as was the rite performed by Moses on Sinai (9,18-21).

The author shows in two complimentary ways that a covenant between God and man cannot be instituted without a sacrificial death. Starting with the Greek word, the literal translation of which would be "arrangement", designating most frequently that which is willed, a last will and testament, the author states that a will has definitive value only after the death of the one who made it. Until that time it is still subject to revision. Obliged to have the stability of a last will, and to withstand all changes, the covenant of the people with God had to be sealed by a death. We understand, therefore, why the ritual of a covenant required a bloody sacrifice (9,16-18).

Another element helps us to understand this situation. Men must have "*clean hands and a pure heart*" (Ps. 24,4) in order to have close intimacy with God. Without expiation for sins and a radical transformation of the sinner, no covenant is possible. Here again, we see the necessity for the shedding of blood for establishing a covenant, or if a covenant be broken, the same necessity for its renewal (9,22).

Accordingly, we see the close connection between the ritual and the covenant and at the same time, that of the priesthood that performs the ritual and the Law that defines the terms of the covenant (7,12). Since the value of a covenant depends on the acts that establish it, the type of covenant will correspond to the character of the sacrificial rite (8,6; 9,1). As we have seen, the sacrifices offered by the ancient priesthood were marked by irremediable exteriority. As a result, they were not apt to establish a flawless covenant (8,7). How could animals used as victims constitute a genuine form of mediation? Certainly, there was an attempt to suggest mediation. The sheep and bulls offered belonged to the people, and, offered in sacrifice, in some sense they then belonged to God. Part of their blood sprinkled on the altar, and another part on the people, in some way united God with the people of Israel. But these rites could not lay claim to any marked efficacy. What bond can there be between man and a slaughtered animal? What bond with God can be forged by a dead animal? These sacrifices had no power to purify man's conscience, to place him in real contact with God.

Therefore, the ancient covenant is imperfect. It lacks inner meaning. In fact, its structure is made up of laws imposed from without, whereas it should draw its vitality from within. The faithful Israelite is imprisoned in a system of minutiae characterized by material prohibitions and prescriptions "*with food and drink and various ablutions*" (9,10); this may afford an apparent security, but in no way does it deliver man from evil. Barely ratified, this old covenant proved to be insufficient (Ex. 32). Later the prophets spoke of its inadequacy and announced a better covenant. Our author quotes at length the most explicit revelation (Jer. 31,31-34; Heb. 8,8-12; 10,16-17). Here the Old Testament testifies against itself in a certain way: *"The days will come, says the Lord, when I will establish a new covenant with the house of Israel and with the house of Judah; not like the covenant that I made with their fathers ..."*

In order to establish a different covenant, it will be imperative to set up a *"wholly different liturgy"* (8,6). Christ did this on Calvary. We have seen already that Christ's Passion is a perfectly interior sacrifice that takes all of man and leads him to God. It must be noted that it is a genuine covenant sacrifice, not because of the effect produced by conventional rites, but because of its profound character. Indeed, the Passion is established on the real existence of a dual relationship: Jesus is the Son of God and the brother of men. The Passion has no objective other than that of carrying out this dual relationship to its ultimate consequences, whatever may be the price. To the very end, Jesus carried out the will of his Father; Jesus manifested the boundless limits of his solidarity with us.

Our natural tendencies lead us to restrict our solidarity with others to the circumstances that are advantageous to us. We do not like our lot to be tied in with that of the unfortunate, particularly if they are so conditioned through their own fault. Jesus, on the contrary, far from limiting his solidarity with us, knowingly and freely accorded it the greatest possible breadth and depth. Having become one of us, a man of flesh and blood (2,14), he was able to bear our pain and to die our death, although he was not constrained to do this, being without sin. He willed, however, to take upon himself the greatest sufferings and a most painful death, the death reserved for criminals (12,2). Thus, his Passion and death sealed his solidarity with us, even with the most guilty among us, and his glorification, which does not nullify his Passion, but shows its value according to the divine plan (2,9), consecrates forever this solidarity, giving to the body of Christ the power to draw to himself multitudes of mankind.

Another element is to be noted. When we state that there is a separation between men and God, we think we are caught in a dilemma: either to range ourselves with men and separate ourselves from God, or, on the other hand, to range ourselves with God and withdraw from men. Not to be divided, we let go one side or the other. Such was not the attitude of Jesus.

Nothing was able to make him compromise either his union with his Father or his ties with us. In him these two fidelities mutually strengthened each other. He found a way of uniting them forever by using the death inflicted on him by sinners (12,13) as a perfect sacrifice offered to God for sin (10,4-10). Let us repeat that this sacrifice that led to the resurrection, to the complete sanctification of renewed human nature, is, at one and the same time, the greatest testimony of fidelity that man has ever rendered to God and the greatest testimony of love that God has ever given men. We cannot imagine any act that would be so truly a covenant sacrifice.

Through it the new covenant is established. Uniting in his glorified body the multitude of believers, Christ grants them a participation in his own union with the Father. These new ties established between God and men have none of the weaknesses found in the ancient covenant. Truly, the cross and the Resurrection have brought about an interior transformation: *"For by a single offering he (Christ) has perfected for all time those who are sanctified"* (10,14).

Thus, the prophecy of Jeremiah that announced a dual change in relation to the former covenant has been realized. On the one hand, the effective forgiveness of sins is granted because the blood of Christ purifies the conscience (9,14). On the other hand, the laws defining the covenant are no longer exterior. In place of being written on stone as formerly (Ex. 32,15-16), God writes them on hearts. That is to say that the new covenant acts within man; by the grace of Christ, the desire to do what pleases God is implanted in man. He has a taste for the good and receives the grace to accomplish it. In this manner a deep harmony is established between God and man: *"this is the covenant that I will make with them after those days, says the Lord; I will put my laws on their hearts, and write them on their minds; I will remember their sins and their misdeeds no more"* (10,16-17; cf. Jer. 31,31-33).

9. THE PRIESTHOOD AND CONTEMPORARY LIFE

In our time several very apparent innovations (the vernacular used for the liturgy, rejection of the traditional clerical costume) have drawn attention to priests. Other changes, less striking but bolder, such as "dialogue with the world", give rise to heated discussions among Christians. Over and above one or more detail, people perceive a concept of the priesthood that they judge either excellent or unacceptable. Some are happy to see the clergy fused with the masses, others deplore "a movement for the vulgarisation of religion and the loss of its sacred character". This controversy may not be useless, if, instead of limiting ourselves to taking sides according to our personal likings, all of us try seriously to deepen our doctrinal knowledge.

The Epistle to the Hebrews is certainly one of the major texts where we must seek for light. Not that it speaks at length of the Christian priest and his vocation; being addressed to the assembly of the faithful, it has only a few words for the "directors" (13,7.17). However, by describing the priesthood of Christ, it throws light on the situation of those who are representatives of Christ's priesthood.

One important point shows up clearly: the author of the epistle realizes that Christ's sacrifice introduces a radical change in the religious condition of humanity. And this change consists in passing from the artificial to the real, from what is exterior to what is all-embracing.

As we have seen, the epistle insists that the ancient religion was marked by irremediable exteriority. Unworthy to present himself before God, man offers the sacrifice of animals. By way of expiation, he uses the animals' blood in conventional rites performed in an artificial sanctuary "made by man" (9,11.24). It is surely possible to see in these rites a certain value. They aim at exciting and expressing concretely a real religious commitment. Yet they were defective expressions, incapable of placing man in communication with God. The Old Testament itself is witness to this (Is. 1,10-15; Ps. 50,13).

Unable to really obtain freedom from evil and union with God, the ritual did nothing more than point up a negative aspect of material separation. The offerings were withdrawn from every day use in order to pass into another area, exteriorly distinct and looked upon as sacred. The deficiency of the sacrifices had its repercussions on all levels of organized religion. Priestly holiness was thought of as an external segregation. In certain families set apart, the priesthood was transmitted from father to son and numerous prohibitions withdrew the priests from ordinary living. In their turn, the people of God were separated and protected from other nations. The Law, binding exteriorly by means of multiple material prescriptions, particularly in relation to food (Heb. 9,10; 13,9), set up sociological barriers that distinguished Jews from pagans.

Such was the ancient condition of religion. The epistle notes that the entire religious system held together: the prescriptions as to food are related to sacrifices (9,10; 13,9); the whole Law is conceived in relation to worship (7,11), so that a change in the priesthood necessarily requires a change in the Law (7,12.18-19). The complete organization of the people of God will be different if a new sacrifice replaces the former offerings.

Christ, by offering himself, put an end to the religion of the Old Testament and its program of external ritual (10,9). Indeed, his sacrifice is not just an episode in his life, it is operative from the moment of his coming into the world until his death on the cross (10,5; 2,14; 12,2). That which gives the full value of sacrifice to Christ's life as man, is precisely his perfect adherence to his Father's will ("Lo, I have come to do thy will, O God", 10,9), an adherence, which during the Passion was not carried out without a dramatic plea (5,7-8).

This adherence led Jesus to bind himself to men and to go to the depths of their distress, in trial, suffering and humiliation (2,10-18; 12,2). On the other hand, it prevents absolutely his accepting a false solidarity that would imply connivance in evil. Christ made himself like to us in all things *save sin* (4,15). If Christ had become our accomplice in evil, his existence would have been without meaning, his death would not have been a sacrifice leading to God and his solidarity with us would have served no purpose other than to have degraded us still more. Through genuine solidarity with men, Christ did not yield before sinners, but "endured from sinners much hostility against himself" (12,3). This brought about his rejection as a criminal by society. Apparently, the cross breaks all the bonds that united Christ to men. In reality, it seals these bonds in a definitive manner, for Christ to the end, receptive to the love coming from the Father, undergoes death with us and for us.

By the same act, all the ancient divisions are abolished. Christ's sacrifice was not an episodic ceremony, unrelated to life, but rather a most real fact, tragically real, the execution of one condemned. Indeed, we cannot imagine any exterior happening that might appear less fit to establish a worship to be paid to God. It is, however, from this dishonoring death that Christ made the perfect offering that introduces human nature into intimacy with God. After that, we do not see any part of man's existence (the doing of evil excepted) that should be excluded from relationship to God.

The separation established between the priest and other men likewise disappears. Christ is not a member of a priestly family and on his cross he is far from fulfilling the requirements of ritual purity! If access to the sanctuary was formerly reserved to the high priest alone, now, on the contrary, all are invited to go forward with assurance by the way Christ opened with his own blood (10,19-20).

Therefore, we must go forward on this new way, the only one that leads to a sure destination. This implies two things. One of these is that, cutting ourselves loose from old concepts, we integrate our religion with our lives, not leaving it on the side-lines. The Christian goes to God through his everyday life and not by conventional observances. The sociological barriers that used to protect Israel no longer have any religious value. Our author declares that security must no longer be sought in them (13,9) and he invites Christians to go "outside the camp" (13,13). The people of God no longer has to hide behind walls; henceforth its route goes through open country. It is by his sound choices, by his manner of facing up to his objective situations, by his way of taking his place in the society where he lives and assuming there his personal responsibilities, be they familial, social, or world-wide, — and this by action or by suffering, — that the Christian is placed in authentic relationship with God, confronted by God's will, and that he must with his brothers approach God and render him service (13,1-6.16.21).

By himself he cannot realize this ideal. Only in the degree that he is united with Christ can he do so. Without this union his life cannot be complete. In place of transforming interiorly the realities of life, he will be carried away by their violence. In place of communicating a spiritual dynamism to his milieu he will allow himself to be permeated with the general inertia. He will not resist sin. He will be unable to discern God's will, or, if discerned, he will not accomplish it. He will not show a genuine solidarity with others. Accordingly, the way is open to us only "*through the blood of Jesus*" (10,19). Christian life is conditioned by the intervention of Christ who speaks to us and unites us to himself by the sacraments.

Let it be noted that the latter are not to be thought of as ritualistic observances. They have no meaning except as modes of uniting our lives with Christ's life. They are indispensable, because without them we are not seen as having "passed into the blood of Jesus" and our life remains defective and unworthy of God. However, they are means; assistance at mass, participation in the liturgy, are not ends in themselves. It is through all the realities of our life and death that we go forward to God, by uniting ourselves with the life and death of Christ. Such is the practice of the fundamental Christian priesthood, that which is common to the entire people of God (Heb. 13,16; Rom. 12,1-2; 1 Peter 2,5).

The place and role of the ministering priesthood entrusted to the clergy of the Church must be understood in this light. This priesthood is sacramental. It constitutes the visible, mediating intervention of Christ in the lives of Christians. Without the ministry of bishops and priests the union between the life of the Christian and Christ's life could not be objectively brought about. All would remain in the realm of subjectivity, which, in fact, is a rejection of mediation.

Therefore, the priestly ministry is indispensable. It is through it that Christ shows objectively his presence and action in the

Church and unites believers to his sacrifice. In order to exercise this ministry priests must, necessarily, be recognized as priests. He who would systematically dissimulate his priesthood would be unfaithful to his vocation. On the other hand, priests must realize that their ministry has no other objective than that of serving the existential priesthood of Christ and of Christians. They are themselves in no way freed from living that existential priesthood. Quite the contrary. In a most urgent manner they are called to unite themselves to the sacrifice of Christ by the genuineness of their lives and to imitate Christ's solidarity with men in order to go forward to God. They are not to adopt a false solidarity that would make them partners in wrong doing were they to adopt the prejudices, the narrowness and the egoism of a given milieu. This false solidarity would erect new barriers and render their apostolate void. More than other Christians, priests have the duty of remaining resolutely open to the designs of God. The sacrifices required of them (celibacy, abstention from certain temporal activities, submission to the Church's authority) are to be understood in this sense; they are not intended to separate them from others; rather, they should make them free for a more universal solidarity. Christ himself shows them this path; he renounced family ties, a temporal kingship and gathered a group of apostles. In this manner he became the perfect highpriest; by solidarity with his brothers "*in all things save sin*", he transformed their lives interiorly, making them the path to salvation.

10. CHRISTIAN LIFE

Hebrews 10,19-25

Christ's oblation results in a radical religious transformation of men because it is a covenant sacrifice. "*On the one hand, a former commandment is set aside because of its weakness and uselessness (for the Law made nothing perfect); on the other hand, a better hope is introduced, through which we draw near to God*" (7,18-19). Concluding his great central explanation, the author describes this new situation in a rich and compact sentence and straightway invites Christians to live their lives in accordance with it: "*Therefore brethren, since we have confidence to enter the sanctuary by the blood of Jesus, by the new and living way which he opened for us through the curtain, that is, through his flesh, and since we have a great priest over the house of God, let us draw near with a true heart in full assurance of faith, with our hearts sprinkled clean from evil conscience, and with our bodies washed with pure water, let us hold fast the confession of our hope without wavering, for he who promised is faithful; and let us consider how to stir up one another to love and good works, not neglecting to meet together, as is the habit of some, but encouraging one another, and all the more as you see the Day drawing near*" (Heb. 10,19-25).

The construction of the sentence in Greek gives rise to discussions, but the principal aspects of the thought are clear. That which, above all, marks the state of the Christian, is the possibility of living in real communion with God. His spiritual life is no longer blocked as it was in pre-Christian life and as it still is for those who do not live in Christ. At that time, as we have seen, access to the sanctuary was prohibited for the people and the priests, and reserved for the high priest alone. Even he was permitted to enter only once a year for a single service, and even that did not constitute real contact with God since it was simply a symbolic ceremony. Before Christ, no man had *"complete self-assurance"* in order to enter the sanctuary and present himself before God.

Let us remark that the Greek term translated by *"complete self-assurance"* does not express the idea of a psychological state of confidence, but an objective situation, a recognized right, a "franchise." Primitively, the term designated the right free men had in their cities to assist at the public assemblies and to speak there. If our condition did not permit this self-assurance in God's presence, it was because we were not free; we were slaves to sin. How could a slave of sin draw near to the all holy God? Therefore, mankind took another direction and went towards the shades of death. This "wage of sin" (Rom. 6,23) confirmed and strengthened our servitude to the prince of death and our withdrawal from the living God.

Now we are admitted to intimacy with God. Our path opens into his light and life. What permits us to pass on this path? *The blood of Jesus.* It was "by his own blood" that Jesus himself entered into the sanctuary (9,12), the sacrifice of his life having elevated his humanity to the glory of the Father. This sacrifice has value for us also. Indeed, this blood was shed for us; it is the *"blood of the covenant."* Yes, *"the God of peace brought again from the dead our Lord Jesus, the great shepherd of the sheep, by the blood of the eternal covenant"* (13,20). Therefore, we, too, may avail ourselves of this blood, or, rather, we may become deeply permeated by this blood that washes sin away and regenerates souls by uniting them to Christ's perfect sacrifice. Sanctified by this blood (13,12), we gain self-assurance in order to present ourselves before God: *"the blood of Christ, who through the eternal Spirit offered himself without blemish to God, shall purify our conscience from dead works to serve the living God"* (9,14).

However, does not death remain an obstacle to our "self-assurance" and our communion with the living God? In the Bible death appears as the demon's mark upon us and it is written that the dead are separated from God (Ps. 88,6). No, we no longer have to fear death, because Christ conquered death and made it into a way. In truth, it is a *"new way,"* opened by his flesh. It is a way marked by paradox; *the wages of sin,* our sufferings and death, have been turned against sin. Christ's death, an act of filial obedience and fraternal love, is a true counterthrust to sin. It obtains pardon and gives admission to true life. Christ used death to "*destroy him who has the power of death, that is the devil,*" and to free us from the slavery in which we were held (2,14-15).

Our death, therefore, is not the worst possible impasse, for, united with the death of Christ, it is a path that leads to our goal. Christ passed through death, but went beyond it. Accepting the rending of his flesh, he procured for it a new and completely transfigured life. That is why the way he opened up is a "*living way.*" It is our way now. Because of the solidarity of Christ's human nature with ours, there where he has passed, our human nature will be able to pass. Indeed, our author gives Jesus the title of the "*pioneer of salvation*" (2,10), and that of "*forerunner.*" "*Jesus has gone as a forerunner on our behalf*" (6,20).

But Christ is more than a forerunner who traces the route to follow, and Christians have more than a way in order to get in touch with God. They have a "*priest,*" a living bond, "*the surety of a better covenant,*" in the very person of Christ (7,22). On the way the distance may still be great between us and the sanctuary; indeed, where are we on this way? But through our priest, we are already in contact with God. Uniting us to his body, Christ has made us "*the house of God,*» at the head of which he is placed as eminent priest, wholly acceptable to God (3,6). Through him and with him, we already have part, really, yet mysteriously, in the blessed life of communion with the Father (3,14; 6,4-5; 12,22-24).

Such is our position in the new covenant, a position that stirs up a feeling of fulfillment and overwhelming gratitude. This gift of God calls for an effective reception in our personal lives. The author calls our attention to this and points out the means to be taken: faith, hope and charity. He states: "*Let us go forward in the fullness of faith, ... let us maintain our unity in hope without weakening ... and let us attend to one another for the strengthening of charity*" (literally, "*for a paroxysm of charity*"). It is through faith, hope and charity that we will be united to our priest and introduced to intimacy with God.

This will not be achieved by a simple mental effort on the part of each one. Faith, hope and charity are planted and nourished in us by Christ's action in the sacramental liturgy. The author is careful to recall, along with faith and hope, baptism, the sacrament of faith and the beginning of hope (cf. Gal. 3,26-29). It is through baptism that "*hearts*" are "*purified*" (the Greek says "sprinkled") when sins are remitted through Christ's sacrifice applied to each one. The rite affects the body that is "*washed with pure water*"; its efficacy, at first interior, will overflow upon the body itself at its resurrection (Rom. 6,3-5). Doubtless, this is why the author speaks here of hope. As for charity, it is connected with the meetings of the Christian assembly, the meetings where the mystery of Christ's body and blood, spoken of in 10,19-20, brings about the union of all in the love that comes from God.

Coming to us through Christ's sacraments, faith, hope and charity are not to be understood as liturgical attitudes without any appreciable role in daily living. Quite the contrary, they can and must transform profoundly the whole fabric of our lives. Faith must not be shut up in a tiny corner of the soul. We must receive its light everywhere, for it is with a "*sincere heart*" that we go forward towards God, "*in the fullness of faith.*" Our lives must manifest "*hope,*" too. It is manifested by an unconquerable strength of soul, which "believes firmly," and regardless of difficulties, continues to hope for salvation from God. Finally, charity cannot be satisfied with illusory feelings; it is shown by "*good works.*"

In these few remarks, the author has pointed up the principal features of Christian life. In so doing, he has recalled earlier exhortations (2,1-4; 3,7 - 4,16; 5,11 - 6,12) and prepared developments to follow; above all, he has shown that everything derives from the same source: the sacrifice and the priesthood of Christ.

11. THE PATHS OF FAITH

Hebrews 3, 4, 11

There is no human existence worthy of the name that has no commitments involving faith. The person who is not willing to go out of himself and have confidence in others will never accomplish a worthwhile work. To establish a home, it is necessary to pledge one's faith forever and to trust for life the word of the other entering into the agreement. What is true of marriage, is true, in differing degrees, of every generous undertaking and of every work done in common. Among men nothing great is ever accomplished without the enthusiasm of faith.

On the plane of the spiritual life, this basic condition is raised to an absolute degree, because it is God with whom we are dealing. When God makes himself known to man in order to associate him with his work in the world, nothing less than complete faith can be asked of him. The divine word stirs up and sustains this faith. Each of us has the fearful possibility of not following its call, of escaping from its action. The Epistle to the Hebrews puts us on our guard against the danger of incredulity and does not grow weary of inviting us to welcome the word of God and to live our faith intensely (3,12 - 4,11; 6,11-12; 10,22; 10,38 - 11,40; 13,7-9).

It is first the existential aspect of faith that is pointed up. *Faith is involvement.* Faith makes decisions and advances to the forefront. Indeed, God's word is not presented as a simple theoretical teaching; it is rather like a program, the announcer of which is God.

In the Epistle to the Hebrews (3,12 - 4,11), the situation of Christians is compared to that of the Israelites when they were close to the land of Canaan. God's word assures them that this is their country and invites them to enter it. "Behold, the Lord your God has set the land before you; go up, take possession, as the Lord, the God of your fathers, has told you; do not fear

4

or be dismayed" (Dt. 1,21). However, the reality does not seem to correspond to this declaration. The country is not an uninhabited land; a race, frightening in appearance, occupies it. A reconnaissance group returns and almost unanimously agrees that the enterprise exceeds the forces of Israel (Dt. 1,22-28; Num. 13,25-33). What will be used as a basis for a decision, the divine statement or the human evaluation? In this instance, the people let themselves become demoralized by the pessimistic reports of the scouts. "You would not go up, but rebelled against the command of the Lord your God" (Dt. 1,26.32). Because they did not believe, God's promise to them was not realized. "And the Lord swore, 'Not one of these men of this evil generation shall see the good land which I swore to give to your fathers'..." (Dt. 1,35; cf. Heb. 3,18-19).

A similar danger still menaces all Christians (Heb. 4,1). The good news has been announced to them as it was to the Israelites in the desert (4,2). The kingdom of God is placed before them with its joy, its peace, all its richness of grace. It is *God's rest* that is open to them. They are invited to enter into it. Will they be able to take a step forward? Or are they going to hold back? If instead of trusting completely the word of God they look for human assurance, their steps will become unsteady and their outlook will be troubled. The ideal they glimpsed will appear illusory and incapable of being lived. It will be a kingdom that cannot be conquered, "a country that devours its inhabitants" (Num. 14,32). Their minds confused, the obstacles grow greater until they become insurmountable: *"the cities are great and fortified up to heaven; and moreover we have seen the sons of giants there"* (Dt. 1,28).

This lack of faith is opposed to the realization of God's promises. Incredulity *"cuts one off from the living God"* (3,12). Then, shut up within himself, spiritually shrivelled, man is unsuccessful. No longer believing that God can and will accomplish great things in him, he turns a deaf ear to grace, and in fact leads a mediocre life. He lives on the sidelines of his vocation. He is deceived by sin (3,13). Finally, his bones strew the desert (Num. 14,29; Heb. 3,17).

The Old Testament does not merely show the deplorable failures caused by lack of faith; it provides also fine examples of authentic spiritual life. Our author does not fail to direct our attention to them and he specifies faith as the unquenchable source of all generous deeds and all graces. Abel and his sacrifice, Henoch and his victory over death, Noah and the ark that brings safety, Abraham and the birth of the people of God, Moses and the departure from Egypt; everything derives from faith, everything is accomplished through faith (11,4-31).

Here also the dynamism of faith is brought to our attention. Believing the word of God, the heroes of faith risked everything for the fulfillment of his plan. They started on their various ways. *"By faith Abraham obeyed when he was called ... and he went out, not knowing where he was to go"* (11,8). Moses, in his turn, *"by faith ... left Egypt, not being afraid of the anger of the king"* (11,27). All the people followed him; *"by faith they crossed the Red Sea"* (11,29). Constantly, faith urges them forward. They do not draw back before any obstacle and succeed in accomplishing seemingly impossible things. Faith brings victory to the most weak and fecundity to the sterile (11,11). The men called by God, *"through faith conquered kingdoms, enforced justice, received promises* (11,33). The prodigies accomplished through faith even included resurrection from the dead (11,35), as the history of Elias and Elisha can testify (1 Kg. 17,23; 2 Kg. 4,36).

These earthly accomplishments are not all. Faith continues its advance. It prevents the faithful ones from sanctimoniously settling themselves in a situation won and calls them to overcome additional difficulties. That is why a list of faith's victories is followed by a list of its trials (11,34-38). *"Mocking and scourging, and even chains and imprisonment,"* such is the lot experienced by God's witnesses. They lead a miserable existence, *"destitute, afflicted, ill-treated."* It seems that faith brings them to ruin and defeat. In reality, it guides them to more decisive victories. To give back life to a child mourned by a grieving mother is assuredly the greatest miracle attributable to faith (1 Kg. 17,22-23; Heb. 11,35). But this earthly miracle, however impressive it may be, has less value than the triumphs of martyrs. *"Refusing to accept release,"* the reward for abjuration, they choose to face death so *"that they might rise again to a better life",* which would fix them forever in intimacy with God (11,35; cf. 2 Macc. 7,9.14). Such are the results of dynamic faith.

What is the source of so strong a faith? The fact that it is a clinging to God by accepting his word. He who relies on God unhesitatingly, participates in his divine stability and power. Accordingly, he is able to accomplish marvels and achieve the impossible (cf. Mk. 9,23; 11,23). In one way, he has already won all. Holding firmly to God's word, the believer, by this very fact, in a mysterious yet real way has everything that word promises. Hence, the affirmation in the epistle: *"Now faith is possession of things hoped for"* (11,1).

At the same time *faith is knowledge,* and this explains its dynamism. The epistle insists on this point. *"Now faith is ... a way of knowing things not seen"* (11,1). Because faith has a long range view, it constantly urges on. It discerns genuine values and, accordingly, endeavors to look beyond more or less illusory ones that attract so much attention. Faith, true knowledge communicated by God's word, and therefore more guaranteed than any other, remains, nevertheless, indirect knowledge that bears upon *"things not seen."*

This certitude, not resting on evidence but on communion with Another, causes the believer to pass through vividly contrasting periods of light and shadow. Now, it is the positive aspect that is discerned. Faith is a *way of knowing;* its mystery illumines everything. At other times, the negative aspect is painfully dominant; *we do not see* what we believe. The believer goes forward in the dark, *"not knowing where he goes"* (11,8). This is good for him. He is being taught by God that there is nothing better for the soul than to rely on him alone. Faith is then strengthened and deepened.

This sort of knowledge can only develop if the whole man is interested in advancing. He who is apathetic cannot receive an increase of light and even risks losing the light he has. Irresolute Christians, instead of becoming teachers, *"need someone to teach them the first principles of God's word"* (5,11-12). The generous believer triumphs over the darkness. His penetrating glance is not obscured by appearances. He is not superficial; being guided by the word of God, he brings to persons and events a penetrating judgment. Brute force does not impress him, nor do riches fascinate him. He knows that spiritual values are not only more beautiful, but also more lasting than material goods. They are the foundation of reality. *"By faith we understand that the world was created by the word of God, so that what is seen was made out of things which do not appear"* (11,3).

Seen in this light, things take on their full meaning; we see them as works of God that deserve our notice (cf. Rom. 1,20). But they lose their borrowed brilliance and we can no longer make them idols. Our eyes having been opened by faith, we are able to be detached from them, following the example of Moses who "*considered abuse suffered for Christ greater wealth than the treasures of Egypt*" (11,26). Such choices astonish the world and even stir up its hostility. As we have seen, the believer does not yield to fear. Moses, "*by faith left Egypt, not being afraid of the anger of the king; for he endured as seeing Him who is invisible*" (11,27).

Invited to imitate such examples, Christians are in a privileged situation (11,40). In their life of faith they are familiar with alternating periods of trial and joy, light and shadow. But they have Christ Jesus, and because of this they experience a fullness that formerly was not obtainable. The ancients received God's word only partially and piecemeal (1,1); for them God's plan was puzzling; they were able only "*to have seen it and greeted it from afar*" (11,13). Through Christ, God expressed himself in a perfect and definitive manner and accomplished perfectly his plan of salvation (1,2-4).

We no longer simply have texts to guide us, we have a living person. The Son of God came to lead us, and walking our ways, he caused them to reach their destination. To go forward with confidence, we need only look "*to Jesus,* the pioneer and perfecter of our faith" (12,2). The mystery of his death and Resurrection reveals to us the meaning of our lives and the value of our sufferings. Thanks to Christ, faith, *a way of knowing,* has become true *spiritual enlightenment* (6,4; 10,32). Thanks to Christ, faith, too, more than ever, is the anticipated possession of fixed rewards. Christ, having entered as a forerunner into glory (6,20), gives us a participation in his "*heavenly gift*" (6,4). We receive "*a kingdom that cannot be shaken*" (12,28); "*for we who have believed enter that rest*" (4,3). Our attention to the word of God must be all the greater and our faith all the more firm and generous. "*Since then we have a great high priest who has passed through heavens, Jesus, the Son of God, let us hold fast our confession*" (4,14).

12. SUFFERING AND HOPE

Hebrews 12,1-13

Saint Isaac Jogues, the French Jesuit missionary in Canada, when a prisoner of the Iroquois, who, after having inflicted horrible tortures on him, made him lead "a life more cruel than any death", turned to Holy Scripture to fortify his endurance. He wrote: It was "my only refuge in the sufferings heaped upon me; I revered it and wanted it with me when I would die. It happened that of all the books we had brought to use with the French living among the Hurons, the only one that fell into my hands was Saint Paul's Epistle to the Hebrews ... I always carried it with me." In his most tragic moments, it was in the Epistle to the Hebrews that he drew strength of soul and unshakeable confidence in God for himself and his companions in suffering. Indeed, this epistle was well written to assist him in overcoming all his sufferings. Addressed to Christians in difficulties, it strengthens them admirably.

Straightway, it gives them courage by recalling their fraternal solidarity with Jesus. We are not alone in our sufferings; Christ came to be close to us, he made himself like to us. He was tried as we are, he suffered, he understands us. *"For we have not a high priest who is unable to sympathize with our weaknesses, but one who in every respect has been tempted as we are, yet without sinning"* (4,15). *"For because he himself has suffered and been tempted, he is able to help those who are tempted"* (2,18). Because of this, for the man who suffers the vise-like grip of solitude is released. In place of being cut off from everyone, even from God, he enters into true communication with the perfect mediator.

Yet, he must accept this mediation and faithfully correspond to it. There is a great temptation to reject *"the complete self-assurance"* (10,35) received in periods of interior illumination.

Failure and suffering have a depressing effect on the soul, particularly if the painful situation is prolonged indefinitely. Doubts come to mind; disappointment and discouragement weaken the will. Balked in its progress towards happiness, enthusiasm under a destructive impulse tends to make an about-face. How believe in joy? There is no such thing as joy. How believe that God loves us? Everything contradicts this idea. Why be generous and put up a fight? Struggle intensifies suffering; it is better to give up and let the soul become numb in darkness.

To these negative thoughts the epistle replies firmly by saying that cowardice is not a solution, that it leads to an impasse and only prepares greater problems. After having received the light of faith and gifts of grace, a Christian who falls away places himself on a blind street (6,4-6). There is no other way to God's peace than the way pointed out by Jesus (3,12-14). There are no remedies for our misfortunes other than the helps his compassion brings us (4,15-16). Against sin that harasses us there is no way of being freed other than through the unique sacrifice of our high priest (10,26). There is only one outlook for him who cuts himself off from Christ: "*a fearful prospect of judgement, and a fury of fire which will consume the adversaries*" (10,27).

After having cut short every attempt of "*evasion*" (10,39), the epistle points out the only open road, that of persevering fidelity. "*For we share in Christ, if only we hold our first confidence firm to the end ...*" (3,14). Each of us must continue to go forward "*in realizing the full assurance of hope until the end*" (6,11); on this road "*you have need of endurance, so that you may do the will of God and receive what is promised*" (10,36).

The epistle is not merely satisfied with directives. It helps us discover the positive meaning of sufferings and their power of enrichment. This knowledge comes to us in the revelation of the mystery of Christ. Jesus could have claimed an earthly life filled with happiness; joy should have been his lot (12,2). However, he chose to endure the cross and in this manner he won glorification for his humanity in the divine intimacy, taking his place at the right hand of God (12,2). Looking at this model, how could we let ourselves be depressed by suffering? The more our lot resembles that of Jesus, the more should we be rooted in confidence. This way is the right way and leads to a destination.

Seen in this light, a passage from Proverbs takes on a rich meaning. The epistle quotes it and comments on it ... *"And have you forgotten the exhortation which addresses you as sons? — 'My son, do not forget lightly the discipline of the Lord, nor lose courage when you are punished by him'"* (12,5). Many of our difficulties are due to the fact that we undervalue trials; we make light of the sufferings God sends us. We have only one anxiety: to get rid of them as soon as possible, because we look only at their disagreeable side and do not wish to see their positive value. If the suffering persists, we become anxious; perhaps we are being weighed in the balance. The thought of our past faults torments us. Or, if we think we have little with which to reproach ourselves, we feel threatened by some mysterious curse. Rebelliousness and discouragement result from this.

These temptations come from a warped point of view. *"Do not lose courage when you are punished by him"* (12,5). Suffering is never a reason for discouragement or lack of confidence in God, since it proves the truth of his love for us: *"For the Lord disciplines him whom he loves, and chastises every son whom he receives."* What light and courage for the faithful one when he hears these words: *"It is for discipline that you have to endure. God is treating you as sons"* (12,7). Suffering being understood as a normal element in life, anxiety disappears. Indeed, our adoption as sons needs to be perfected by the educative action of suffering.

When suffering comes we should not be troubled. It would be alarming did it not come. *"If you are left without discipline, in which all have participated, then you are illegitimate children and not sons"* (12,8). Isaac Jogues and his companions understood this very well. Aware of the pain that was to be theirs, they said: "Knowing that if we withdraw from those who are scourged, we would also be withdrawing from the number of his sons, we offered ourselves with generous hearts to our God who chastises as a father, so that he might be pleased with us as with his sons." When we surrender ourselves with this generosity to the action of grace, suffering assumes a different mien. Instead of having the unfeeling aspect of fate that strikes and destroys, it lets something of love and light shine through. Its painful coming turns out to be beneficent.

In order to have its readers appreciate better the divine pedagogy, and not without a touch of humor, the epistle recalls an experience of family living. As children, we have all been corrected by our parents and the corrections were effective; our conduct improved. *"We have had earthly fathers to discipline us and we respected them. Shall we not much more be subject to the Father of spirits?"* He wishes to give us something more and better than good manners, the gift of fullness of life. Yes, thanks to him, *"we will live"* (12,9).

Without wishing to undervalue familial education, its limitations must be recognized. Often parents are satisfied with superficial aims; even those most eager to fulfill their parental role are only able to act in an approximate way. The interior growth of their child is a mystery to them. They correct *"at their pleasure"* (12,10). Our heavenly Father has great ambitions for us. His love wills nothing less than that *"we may share his holiness"* (12,10). To this end what depths may not his action reach? It is understood only after having been experienced. We would be wrong, were we to get disturbed beforehand. God knows what is best for each one of us. It is for our good that he intervenes (12,10). Instead of becoming paralyzed by looking steadily at obstacles in our way, we must look confidently towards the goal to which our Father is leading us. *"For the moment all discipline seems painful rather than pleasant; later it yields the peaceful fruit of righteousness to those who have been trained in it"* (12,11).

Ultimately, far from ruining Christian hope, suffering is advantageous for it; it is even necessary. Without it, hope would be vague, an ill defined yearning for happiness. Through difficulties it takes on the character of a genuine, personal relationship with God (cf. Rom. 5,3-6; Jas. 1,2-4). The faithful Christian learns then what it means to count on God (2 Cor. 1,8-10). Following Jesus Christ in his mystery of suffering and glory (Heb. 12,1-2; 1 Pet. 4,12-13), he experiences in his own life the victorious action of a very loving Father who shares his holiness with each of his sons.

13. CHARITY AND HOLINESS

Hebrews 12,14 - 13,21

Wishing to point out to the members of the Christian community the *"straight paths"* (12,13) that will really lead them to their objective, the author of the epistle goes back to Psalm 34: *"Seek peace and pursue it."* He adds two details. One has to do with the neighbor. "Pursue," says he, "peace *with all*" (12,14). Thus, it is not a question of attaining peace by means of selfish isolation. We cannot be at peace *with all* except by sharing in common efforts and common joys, taking on the same cares and anxieties, in a word, by living in harmony and love. The second detail has to do with our dealings with God. Along with peace it is necessary to pursue *"holiness, lacking which, no one will see the Lord"* (12,14). Unless governed by this most basic objective, the seeking for good relationships with others could degenerate into an attitude of withdrawal, which, however attractive its passing advantages might be, would be very prejudicial. The last section of the epistle, where the concepts of holiness and love are fused as one, supports this view.

Indeed, a brotherly solidarity in the pursuit of a common ideal is the mark of a Christian community. The epistle never presents our progress towards God as an effort of isolated individuals. Together *"we have"* a high priest (4,14-15; 10,21). Together we constitute *"his house"* (3,6), united as we are in the *"new covenant"* established in the blood of his sacrifice (9,15). Far from disrupting human solidarity, by assuming it Jesus strengthened it, and by becoming our brother he forged new bonds with us (2,11-12). *We share in Christ* (3,14), and we are called to go together towards God. The epistle does not use the singular form, "draw near to God." It says and repeats, using the plural: *"Let us then with confidence draw near to the throne of grace ... let us draw near with a true heart in full assurance of faith ... and let us consider how to stir up one another to love and good works"* ... (4,16; 10,19-25). The call to holiness comes to us not singly, but along with others, and is, accordingly, inseparable from love.

Let us remark that the very call to holiness gives love its full consistancy. This aspect is often ignored and explains why our love of neighbor remains on a sadly superficial level. If one deeply loves another, how can he be satisfied by wishing him a comfortable, yet insignificant life? This would be comparable to loving a person as one loves a dog or cat. For one whom we truly love we desire great things, a full life, during which he may reach his full stature and accomplish completely that for which he was created. Thus considered, it is clear that we could not wish for anyone a better thing than the full realization of his spiritual vocation.

Therefore, true Christians help one another as much as they can to accept generously God's graces. Repeatedly, our author urges this brotherly interest of one for another. Starting with chapter three, he incites our watchful attention: *«Take care, brethren, lest there be in any of you an evil, unbelieving heart, leading him to fall away from the living God. But exhort one another every day, as long as it called 'today', that none of you may be hardened by the deceitfulness of sin"* (3,12-13). Further on, he expresses anxiety inspired by love: *"Therefore, while the promise of entering his rest remains, let us fear lest any of you be judged to have failed to reach it"* (4,1). His objective is to stir up generosity: *"Let us therefore strive to enter that rest, that no one fall by the same sort of disobedience"* (4,11). In the last chapters, he insists on the same ideas. He invites the Christians to *"see to it that no one fails to obtain the grace of God"* (12,15). The entire community is responsible for each of its members and its sollicitude must touch on what is essential, namely, on each one's fidelity to God's call.

The apostle himself practices this type of love. He tries to make the faithful more conscious of their vocation and their position as Christians, a privileged vocation, very different from the ancient religious situation (12,18-24). He stresses the demands that result from complete fidelity (12,25-29). The kind of love shown them by the apostle cannot weaken them. On the contrary, it encourages total self-giving in obedience and love in union with the sacrifice of Jesus (13,12-17). The last wish expressed in the epistle is that God may give Christians, through Jesus Christ, the grace *"to do his will"* (13,21). To appreciate the significance of this expression, it would be sufficient to read again the passage in chapter ten where Christ, *"coming into this world"* offers himself *"to do the will"* of his Father. This offering of himself orientates him toward the filial obedience of the Cross, the perfect realization of God's plan. The apostle wishes his Christians to share in this expendability and sacrifice. His ambition in their regard will be satisfied only when they are willing, if need be, in their *struggle against sin to resist to the point of shedding blood* (12,4). The stronger and more genuine their love, the more will it be imbued with a longing for holiness.

It must not be thought that this love should proscribe all signs of tender affection and become a stoical harshness. When they wish their brothers great courage in difficulties, they are, none the less, eager to help them. In all circumstances, *"let brotherly love continue"* (13,1) and let it be seen by deeds. The apostle congratulated the faithful in these words: *"God is not so unjust as to overlook your work and the love which you showed for his sake in serving the saints, as you still do"* (6,10). He recalled the part they played in the sufferings of the Church: *" sometimes being publicly exposed to abuse and affliction, and sometimes being partners with those so treated. For you had compassion on the prisoners ..."* (10,33-34). He concludes by recommending that they persevere in the same attitude: *"Remember those who are in prison, as though in prison with them; and those who are ill-treated, since you also are in the body"* (13,3). The more their compassion is sincere and their devotedness generous, the more will they be united with their high priest, *"merciful and trustworthy"* (2,17).

The decisive factor in the relationship between holiness and love is the sacrifice of Jesus. In one and the same action, Jesus brought about the complete offering of himself to God and the total gift of self to men. Thus he brought about the perfect synthesis of holiness and love. Any attempt aiming at separating one from the other would constitute an unwise retrogression. Our author cautions us about *"diverse and strange teachings"* (13,9) that might bring about this division. In his great central exposition, he showed that the former methods of sanctification were not efficacious (9,9-10; 10,1-4) and that they were definitively replaced by the sacrifice of the new covenant. In concluding the epistle, he is careful to show the changes that result in relation to the worship of Christians.

The ancient "holiness," as we have already shown, consisted in exterior rituals that set apart the people of God. Separated from pagans by numerous legal barriers, Israel was a closed society. Christian holiness does not adapt itself to these conditions. To bring about this holiness, Jesus did not remain inside the camp. *"So Jesus ... suffered outside the gate in order to sanctify the people through his own blood"* (13,12). As a result, Christians are to reject the barriers of the former cult. Henceforth, holiness is not to be sought in laws regarding food, nor in rules appertaining to ritual purity (Heb. 13,9). To persist in attributing an absolute value to these practices would be to shut themselves up again in the *"camp"* with *"those who serve the tent"* (13,10), and at the same time to give up participating in the sacrifice of Christ.

Authentic worship no longer consists in exterior options; it adopts new forms in which fraternal charity and enthusiasm for the things of God mutually favor each other. On the one hand, Christians are called upon to offer God through Christ perpetual thanksgiving: *"Through him (Jesus) then let us continually offer up a sacrifice of praise to God"* (13,15). On the other hand, they are called to live in effective love: *"Do not neglect to do good and to share what you have, for such sacrifices are pleasing to God"* (13,16). It is evident that the worship of God and love of neighbor are closely linked. Thanksgiving rises to God, but being communal, it welds, more than any other activity, those who take part in it. A life of love affects immediately relationships with the neighbor, but at the same time it is understood as an offering to God, an act of adhesion to the dynamic movement of his love. This movement fixes no limits. Love seeks to expand, thanksgiving seeks only to receive new participants. It is thus that the Christian Church, united in the faith preached by its *"first directors"* (13,7-9) and in docility to their successor (13,17) realizes progressively the ideal proposed to it, the ideal of *"peace among all and holiness"*, so as to prepare *"to see the Lord"*.

CONTENTS

TIPOGRAFIA DELLA PONTIFICIA UNIVERSITÀ GREGORIANA — ROMA